The Guardian of the Forest

(An Owl Story)

Sandeep Kumar Mishra

Title-

The Guardian of the Forest: An Owl Story

Author -

Sandeep Kumar Mishra

Illustrations-

Harish Verma

Publisher

Kishlaya Books

October, 2024

About the Author

Sandeep Kumar Mishra's accolades include the "Vedvyas Award-2022", "Poiesis Award-2022", "Readers Favorite Award-21", "Indian Achievers Award-21", "IPR Poetry Award-2020" and "Literary Titan Book Award-2020"." among others.

His work has been shortlisted for prestigious awards such as 'Page Turner Book Award-2024', "The Next Generation Story Award-2024", "Plough Poetry Prize-2024", "Fish Poetry Prize-24", Short Story Unlimited-2024", "2023 Commonwealth Story Prize," "2021 International Book Awards," and "52nd New Millennium Award-2021,"MPT Story Award-2022' and 'Newcastle Story Award-2022" and "Anasi Story Award-2022" and "Independent Press Award-2022" and "IAN Book Award 2022"

More information-

https://www.sandeepkumarmishra.com

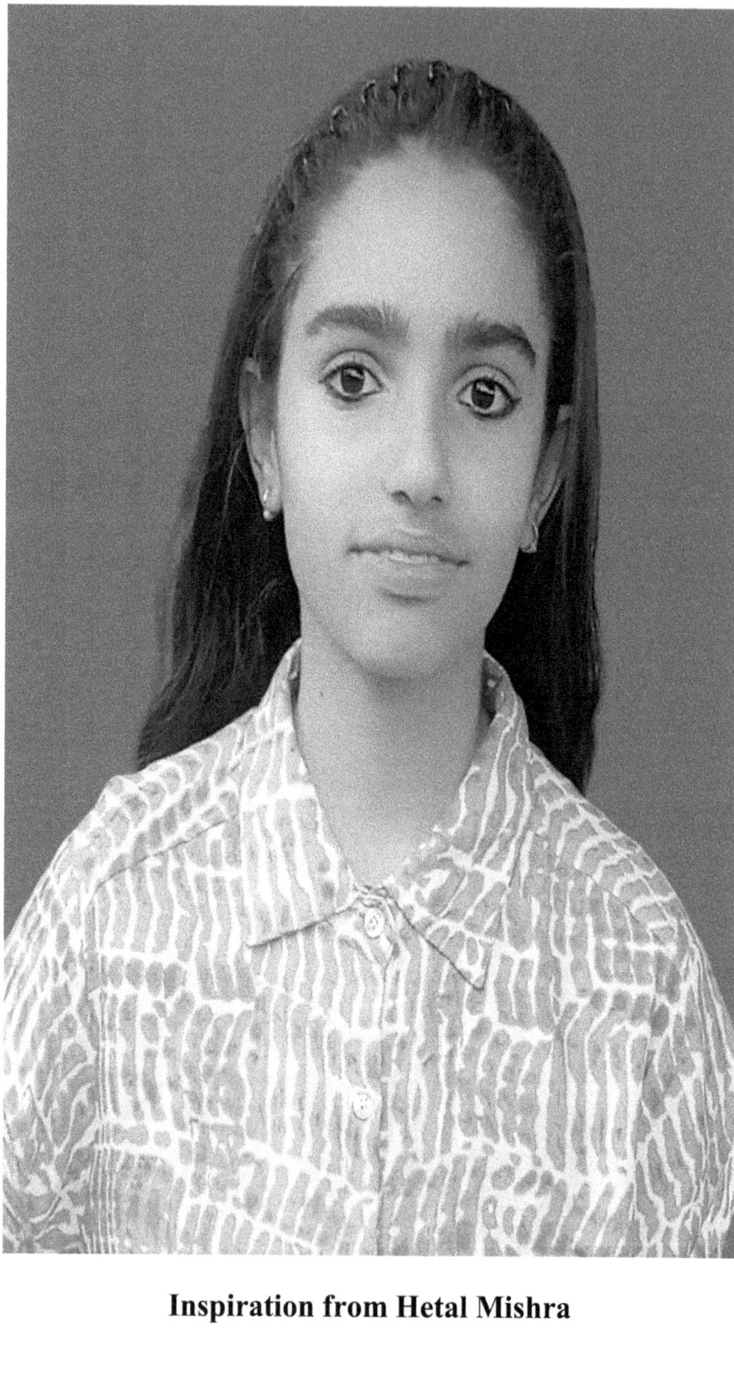

Inspiration from Hetal Mishra

The Guardian of the Forest: An Owl Story

It's been a week now. Every night they have heard a strange hooting sound coming from the forest nearby. The sound was mysterious and captivating. Determined to uncover its origin, the animals convened for a discussion.

Tina, the wise horse, spoke first. “My dear friends, have you all heard that strange hooting sound coming from the forest lately?”

Leela, the energetic duck, nodded eagerly. "Yes, Tina! It's been echoing through the trees, and I can't help but wonder what creature could be making such a sound."

Vimal, the brave rabbit, added, "It's not like any owl I've ever heard before. It's as if it carries a secret message or a hidden meaning."

Somu, the clever dog, smirked and chimed in, "Well, my friends, I believe it's up to us to solve this mystery. We should venture into the forest and investigate the source of the hooting sound."

Tina nodded in agreement. "Indeed. We must exercise caution and work together. Safety in numbers, as they say."

Excitement flickered in Leela's eyes. "I'm ready to explore the unknown! Let's go and find out what lies within the depths of that forest!"

With their decision made and filled with a sense of adventure and curiosity, the animals made their way toward the forest to find the source of the hooting sound. With every step they took, their anticipation grew.

Somu led the way, his sharp senses alert to any signs of danger. "Stay close, everyone. We don't know what awaits us."

Vimal hopped nervously, glancing around. "Could it be a magical owl? One that possesses ancient knowledge or even grants wishes?"

Tina's wise voice soothed the rabbit's anxiety. "Let's not jump to conclusions, my friend. We must approach this with an open mind and remain observant."

As they journeyed deeper, the forest grew darker and an eerie silence settled around them. The towering trees blocked the moonlight, making it difficult for them to see, Leela was more frightened than others. She claimed she could see eyes in the trees.

“What’s that? Who's there?” Leela said into the darkness.

“Where?” asked Vimal.

“Over there. Can’t you see it? There are eyes everywhere” replied Leela, “I should have stayed in my lovely pond” she cried out.

“Leela. Whatever is in there would get you and have for dinner,” said Somu

Chuckling, Tina said, "Cut it out Somu, nothing is coming to get her, not while you're here. Calm down, Leela! There's nothing in here, and if there is, Somu here will protect you."

This made Leela a bit calm. Despite the ominous ambiance, their determination kept them going. The hooting grew louder, guiding them to its source. After what felt like an eternity, they arrived at a hidden clearing bathed in moonlight. Perched on a branch above them was a beautiful and majestic owl, larger than any they had ever seen.

The owl's feathers shimmered in the moonlight, casting an ethereal glow. Its eyes shone with mystery and wisdom; the animals gazed up in awe feeling a sense of reverence for the mystical creature. Sensing their presence, the owls spoke in a gentle voice. "Welcome brave adventurers."

The animals were taken aback by the owl's unexpected ability to communicate, but Tina stepped forward, "Who are you, wise owl?" Tina inquired, "And what brings you to our meadow?"

"I am Roohi, the guardian of the forest. The hooting sound you heard was my call for help." replied the owl.

Confused, Leela asked, "But why would you need help, you seem so powerful and wise."

Roohi sighed, her eyes filled with sadness. "I indeed possess great power and wisdom, but what is that compared to the gift of flight?"

“We do not understand Roohi, what do you mean?” Tina asked.

“I have always been earthbound, unable to fly like my companions,” Roohi explained.

Vimal the brave rabbit stepped forward, “We can help you, Roohi! Together we can find a way to fulfill your wish.”

Somu, the clever dog said, “Yes! We'll seek out the ancient wise old owl rumored to be in the depths of this forest. It is said he knows the answers to every question, and no problem is so difficult that he cannot solve it. If anyone can unlock the secret of flight, it’s him.”

“Thank you so much, brave adventurers," Roohi said happily, filled with hope that she too would fly soon.

Determined, the animals began their adventure into the thicker parts of the forest in search of the ancient owl. The forest guided them through thick and dark paths, where they could barely see the glow of the moonlight and overrunning streams. After a long, difficult, and exhausting journey, they came to a small clearing, where the ancient owl was said to reside.

Looking closely, perched on a branch was an owl even more majestic than Roohi named Garuda.

“Who dares disturb my domain?” the owl hooted in a melodic yet strong voice.

"We apologize for intruding noble owl, we come in need of your great wisdom and knowledge," replied Somu.

"And how may I help you?" Garuda asked.

"Our friend Roohi seeks the gift of flight," replied Leela.

"Is Roohi a rabbit?" asked Garuda.

"No, she is not, she is an owl," replied Leela.

"But she is an owl, how is it she cannot fly?" asked Garuda perplexed.

"She has always been earthbound, and has never known how to fly," replied Leela.

With a thoughtful gaze, he said, “The secret of flight lies not in wings, but in the courage to embrace change.”

Intrigued, Tina asked, “What do you mean Garuda?”

He continued, “To fly, Roohi must first believe in herself, shed her doubts, and trust in her abilities. Only then will she discover the freedom she seeks.”

Armed with newfound insight, the animals returned to Roohi. They relayed Garuda’s words and Roohi’s eyes were filled with newfound determination.

With each passing day, Roohi practiced spreading her wings and soared from branch to branch. She faced her fears head-on, embracing the courage she had found within.

Slowly her flight improved, until one day she took to the skies, gliding gracefully among the treetops.

News of Roohi's triumphant flight spread throughout the forest. The animals rejoiced, celebrating her newfound freedom. Roohi's hooting sound became a joyous melody, a symbol of courage and perseverance. The hooting sound no longer remained a mystery but became a testament to the power of belief and the beauty of embracing change.

******

True freedom comes from believing in yourself and embracing courage

www.ingramcontent.com/pod-product-compliance
Ingram Content Group UK Ltd.
Pitfield, Milton Keynes, MK11 3LW, UK
UKHW021410190726
13845UKWH00028B/1010

9 789334 138306